THIS BOOK IS DEDICATED IN LOVING MEMORY OF

CHARLEY HARPER

1922-2007

WITH HEARTFELT THANKS TO
EDIE HAPER, BRETT HARPER, AND TODD OLDHAM

A IS FOR APE

B

IS FOR BIRD

C
IS FOR CRAB

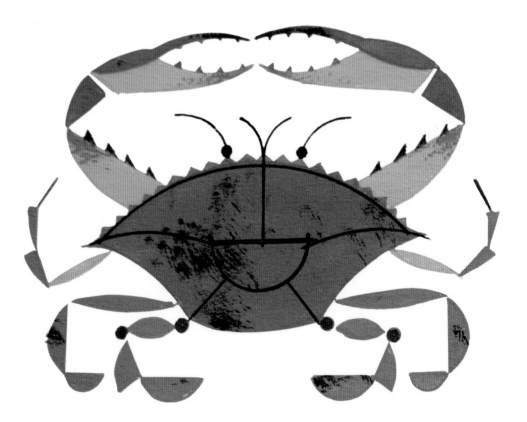

D IS FOR DOG

E IS FOR ELEPHANT

F IS FOR FROG

G IS FOR GIRAFFE

H

IS FOR HEN

I IS FOR IGUANA

J IS FOR JELLYFISH

K

IS FOR KOALA

L

IS FOR LADYBUG

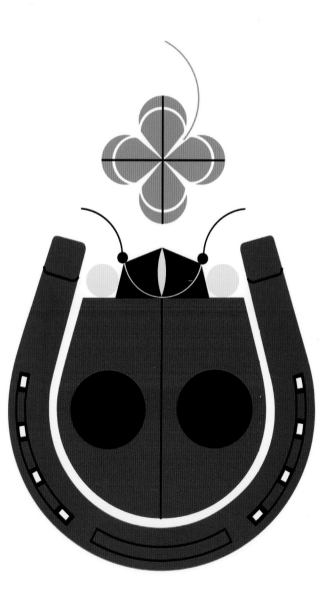

M IS FOR MONKEY

N IS FOR NEST

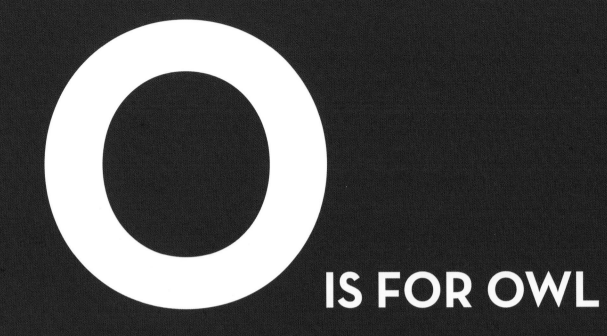

IS FOR OWL

P

IS FOR PIG

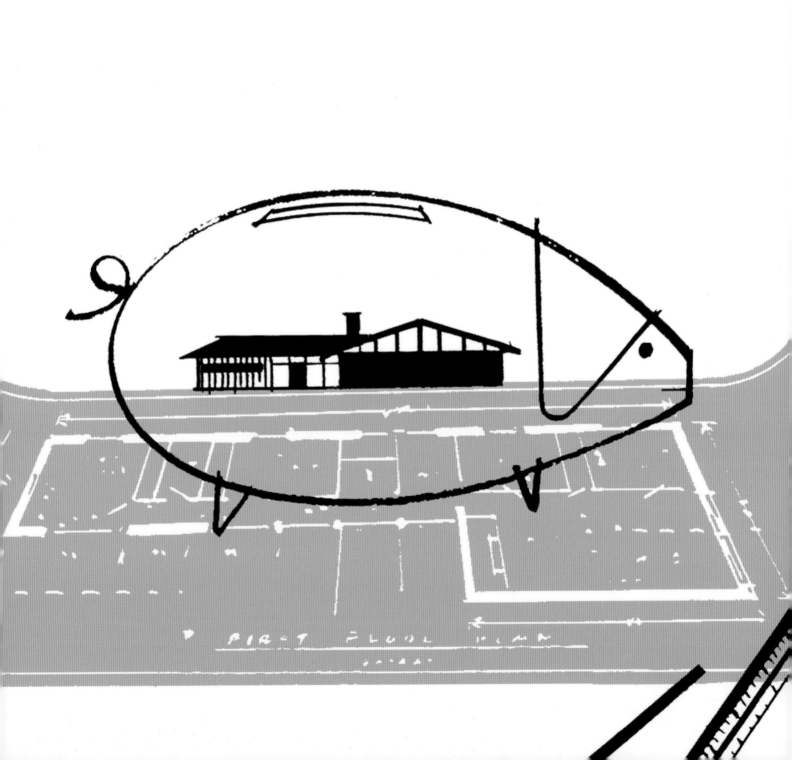

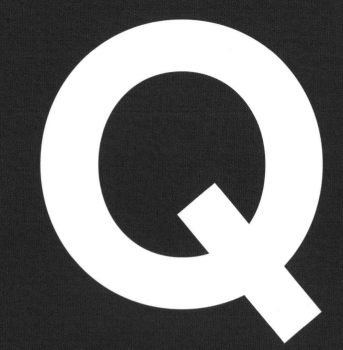 IS FOR QUAIL

R IS FOR RABBIT

S

IS FOR SNAIL

T
IS FOR TURTLE

U

IS FOR
UNDERWATER

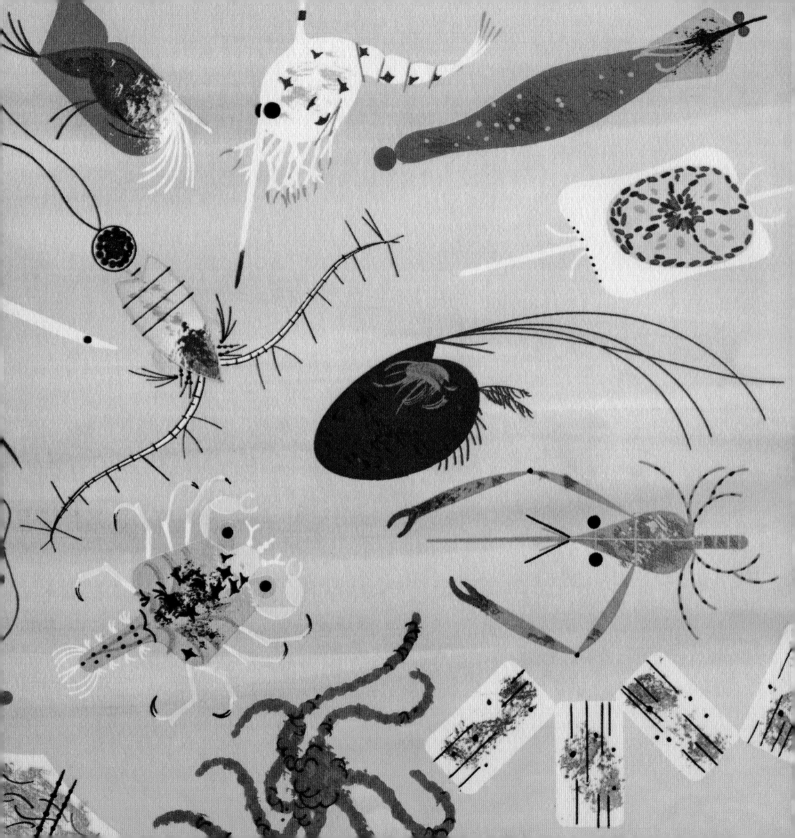

V IS FOR VULTURE

W

IS FOR WEB

X

HOW MANY X'S
CAN YOU FIND ?

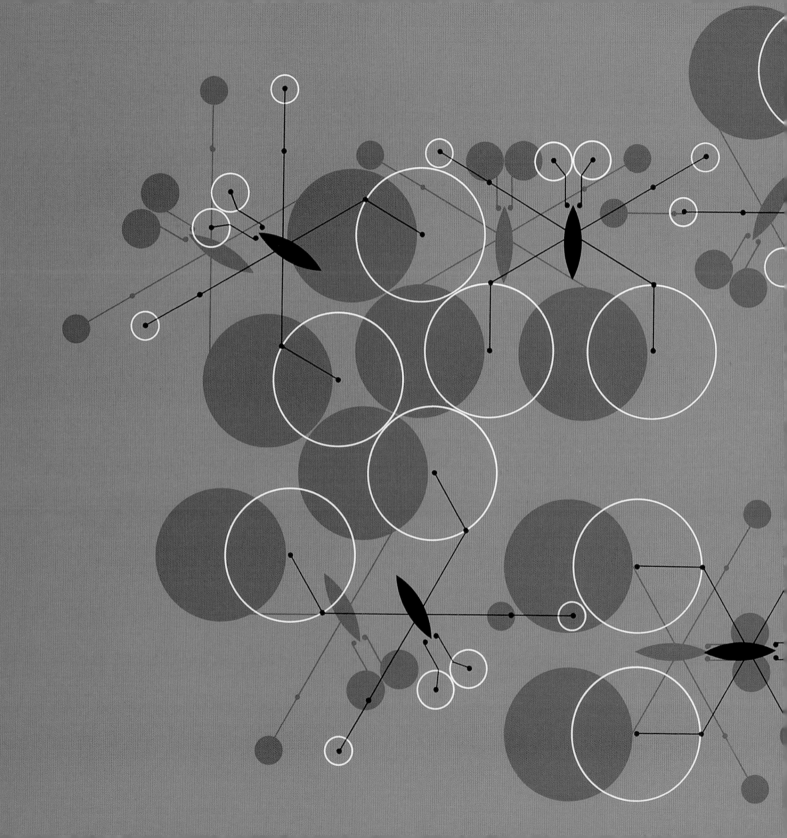

Y IS FOR YAK

Z IS FOR ZEBRA

CHARLEY HARPER

1922- 2007

Ever since he was a young boy growing up on a farm, Charley Harper loved animals and enjoyed drawing and painting pictures of them. For over 60 years, Charley painted beautiful, colorful, and graphic paintings of nature, animals and the world around him. Birds, insects and many other creatures visited him everyday in the woods behind his home studio in Cincinnati, Ohio.

DESIGN: GLORIA FOWLER
SPECIAL THANKS TO STEVE, MILES, AND LOLA CRIST

FOR MORE CHILDRENS BOOKS AND PRODUCTS VISIT US AT:
WWW. AMMOBOOKS.COM

AMMO